LOVE
FEED
SPUR
CONNECT

God's engine for His Church and purpose for our lives.

alan scott

© 2025 by Alan Scott and Lifebridge Community Church.

All rights reserved. No part of this publication may be reproduced in any form without written permission from the author and Lifebridge Community Church, 3102 Loring Rd., Kennesaw, GA 30152. www.lifebridgecommunity.com

Due to the challenging nature of the internet, if there are any web addresses, links, or URLs included in this manuscript, these may have been altered and may no longer be accessible. The views and opinions shared in this book belong to the author and Lifebridge Community Church.

Contents

Preface	i
Introduction	1
Chapter One	15
Love People One At A Time	
Chapter Two	35
Feed People The Word of God	
Chapter Three	49
Spur People To Serve	
Chapter Four	71
Connect People To God Through Prayer And Worship	
Author's End Note	87
About the Author	91

Preface

Lifebridge Community Church's history began in 2011 when Jeff Bennett and Aaron Gable joined forces to plant a thriving church in Kennesaw/Acworth, Georgia. The original mission statement was: *"Lifebridge is a safe place to explore faith and follow Jesus. Our purpose is to bridge the gap for each other from where we are to where God wants us to be."*

By 2013, space at 3102 Loring Rd. was leased; by 2016, it had been purchased.

A tragic loss occurred in May of 2016. A key elder/leader, John Wernowsky, and his son Jake died in a horrific boating accident. This massive emotional blow to the body of Lifebridge became the impetus for birthing the Women's Tiny Home ministry of J & J Village – located at the back of Lifebridge's property.

By 2018, through a giving campaign called "Hero Maker," Lifebridge had helped fund an Ecuador church plant and launched Creekside Church in Paulding County, GA. The energy, leaders, finances, and people removed from Lifebridge to begin Creekside were Kingdom-worthy efforts but left a difficult void for those who remained.

In 2019 and 2020, a season of pastoral exhaustion was mixed with COVID and a failed merger attempt. This challenging season pushed Lifebridge to the brink and to a critical leadership retreat in Spring 2022.

The March 4-5 leadership retreat resulted in a hard evaluation and honest assessment. Some sixty leaders attended. Out of the ashes came several teams to address "what's important now." A prayer team, a small groups/discipleship team, a communication team, a pathway team, and a vision/mission team were born.

After months of intense work and study through the entirety of the New Testament, the vision/mission team unpacked key ideas and scripture to help give direction to Lifebridge. After putting their work into the hands of the elders and staff, a new vision (what we want to become) was formed: **"We are Gospel-Driven. Together."**

The graphic below highlights the many layers of depth and meaning, pointing back to the newly formed vision.

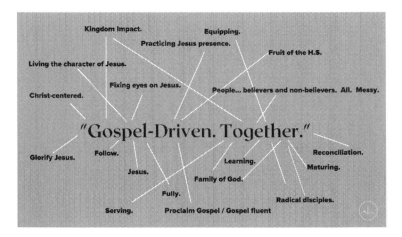

With a new vision that would serve as a mighty rallying cry, the mission (how to accomplish the vision) became of utmost importance.

Taking cues from Acts 2:42, Lifebridge landed on the four-pronged Biblical mission to love, feed, spur, and connect. Lifebridge will accomplish her vision by working out the mission of 1) Loving people one at a time, 2) Feeding people the Word of God, 3) Spurring people to serve, and 4) Connecting people to God through prayer and worship. We call these our 4 Pistons and the engine of God's Church.

This book is a practical guide and working manual explaining how these four pistons work together. As you sort through universal church struggles, consider Biblical solutions, and understand the practical application of love, feed, spur, and connect – you will see how you fit into the bride of Christ at Lifebridge.

There is a necessary disclaimer that seems fitting at the outset. With everything you're about to read, please understand that we don't have it down perfectly. We are a work of God in progress. Some ideas presented in this book we crush (in a good way); others not so much. Some things may change or be tweaked, but the foundational Biblical principles remain. A few ideas promoted are inspirational and looming on the horizon. Please know that without God, His Spirit, and His people, there is absolutely nothing we can do. But WITH Jesus, all things are possible! Even a strong, healthy, growing church can emerge.

May God bless you on your journey. Your investment in learning how to love, feed, spur, and connect better is a good expenditure of time. Our church mission could become your mission and purpose. Ultimately, we hope you will join Lifebridge Community Church in becoming Gospel-driven. Together.

Introduction

Be careful how you answer this next question. It's probably a good idea to place your mechanic on speed dial with such a potentially damaging inquiry. Here it goes...

How well is your car running right now?

If you say, "good," watch out! You've jinxed your current carefree season as you "head out on the highway, looking for adventure."

Typically, when your car is humming and purring, you don't usually put much thought into the pistons and cylinders that get you down the road.

Nobody thinks about their car's engine when it's running well. As with our teeth, refrigerator, flatscreen, and internet modem – you don't think about how something works until it doesn't.

For many, church hasn't worked in a long time. Why is that? Church leaders and volunteers seem deeply dedicated to Jesus. Most church people want their churches to thrive and grow. Why are there so many congregations struggling with a flatline plateau or decline?

The number of burned-out, frustrated, and confused church leaders and volunteers is not insignificant. A compulsory look at the first-century church found in the New Testament can frustrate current church people even more. Comparatively, why aren't more churches today as healthy, dynamic, and growing naturally as the church was in the book of Acts?

What engine drove the New Testament church we observe within the pages of scripture? How did that incredible engine work, and are all those same pistons firing in our church today?

Many engines have been tried and failed. The seeker-targeted, purpose-driven, missional, and house church engines have all been revved but still have been left wanting. Nothing seems sustainable, having stood the test of time, cultural shifts, and endless church growth conferences.

Is there a Biblical engine we should be aware of? Throw me the keys to that puppy!

Take a look at Ephesians 4:11-13.

"So Christ himself gave the apostles, the prophets, the evangelists, the pastors, and teachers, to equip his people for works of service, so that the body of Christ may be built up until we all reach unity in the faith and in the knowledge of the Son of God and become mature, attaining to the whole measure of the fullness of Christ."

Wow. Ephesians 4 unpacks breathtaking ideas about Jesus' Church. Dynamic, healthy, growing churches must be possible, or this Bible passage is a cruel joke. Why would God dangle such an incredible congregational carrot if it wasn't possible, or greater yet, God's will?

In the early church, the work of ministry was done by the people, not just the leaders. The New Testament church featured leaders who trained the people to do ministry work. Whaaa da what?

In many modern churches, the paid, professional staff usually does the work of ministry. The staff works incredibly hard, and the members put money in the giving boxes and watch the staff work.

How's that been going for us? There is no comparison when you compare the modern church to Ephesians 4:11-13.

How have things sunk to this level of low for the Western church? Are we afraid to unleash messy volunteers? Do church members feel inadequate compared to the professionals? Do the professional staff people not want others to help with the work? Maybe the paid people believe they can do the job better because they're better trained.

The Flintstones is an ancient, stone-age cartoon show reserved for Saturday mornings of old. Fred and Wilma Flintstone were neighbors with Barney and Betty Rubble. Fred and Barney were also best buds working for Bedrock Quarry and Gravel Company. Barney would typically grab a ride to work with Fred. Fred's engine was powered by feet – his. If Fred's feet were tired, so went the car. If Fred had a blister or broken toe, the car didn't run. You get the picture: no feet, no engine, no car. The Flintstone mobile would only go as far as Fred's feet would carry it.

Are churches today powered only by their lead pastor? Isn't that, in reality, a Fred Flintstone mobile? Such a church will go only as far as the pastor who carries it. That doesn't sound good, and it isn't. Too many stories of fallen, broken pastors result in fallen, broken congregations.

With a magnifying glass on the first-century church found in the book of Acts, we see a different model unfold. Perhaps what we see is God's design and engine for His church. There's a novel idea!

And let's be very clear: the fuel in the tank and oil in the engine of God's church in Acts was the supernatural work of the Holy Spirit. Jared Wilson writes, "...the soul can only be changed by supernatural power. And there is only one place the pastor can find supernatural power – the Spirit of God working through the message of the Gospel, the finished work of the Son of God."[1] This dynamite dynamic of the Holy Spirit in the first-century church is undeniable and worthy to be noted.

Take a look at Acts 2:42-47. Reread it as if never seen before. Discover God's design for His church, perhaps for the very first time.

"They devoted themselves to the apostles' teaching and to fellowship, to the breaking of bread and to prayer. Everyone was filled with awe at the many wonders and signs performed by the apostles. All the believers were together and had everything in common. They sold property and possessions to give to anyone who had need. Every day they continued to meet together in the temple courts. They broke bread in their homes and ate together with glad and sincere hearts, praising God and enjoying the favor of all the people. And the Lord added to their number daily those who were being saved."

---

1 Jared C. Wilson, Gospel Driven Ministry, (Zondervan 2021, Grand Rapid, MI) pg. 28.

The early church had an incredibly efficient 4-piston engine. They focused on a few things. The Christians in Jerusalem were:

1. **Bible-based.** They devoted themselves to the Apostles' teaching. What was the teaching? Jesus. The Gospel. The good news. The death, burial, and resurrection of Jesus. Creation, Fall, Redemption, and Restoration. God created a perfect world with shalom, peace, and void of sin. There was no death, brokenness, or goodbyes. Imagine that. It was a breathtaking creation.

   But Adam and Eve listened to the whispers of Satan, who said, "Did God really say...?" We still hear the same whispers today. "Did God really say you couldn't eat from any tree?" "Did God really say you couldn't be happy?" Did God really say you couldn't do everything you want to do?" "Did God really say...?" Adam and Eve ate the banana from the one tree God said they couldn't eat from. Suddenly, they knew what evil was. Now they knew what sin was. Now they knew they were naked and hid from an all-knowing God. How ridiculous is that? And when Adam and Eve disobeyed God, perfection was broken. We call this the Fall. Sin, death, disease, struggle. Life separated from God became a reality for us all.

   But God... those are such great, hope-filled words. But God immediately pursued Adam and Eve. He covered their nakedness with animal skins – which meant blood had to be shed to cover over their sin. This is the Bible's first image of Jesus, who shed his blood to cover our sin. We call this redemption. Redemption means God repurchases us. Incredible. He made us; we are His. We walk away, and he buys us back. How much love and sacrifice does that take? Wow.

Ultimately, God aims to bring His creation shalom, peace, and healing. Soon, a new heaven and earth will be without sin, death, disease, and goodbyes. This is restoration.

Creation, Fall, Redemption, Restoration.

The Apostles regularly taught this good news. This was the message. This was what their teaching centered on. Billy Graham's grandson, Tullian Tchividjian, is noted as saying, "Jesus plus nothing equals everything." THAT was the Apostles' teaching, and the first-century church remained focused on it. They were devoted.

The Apostle Paul continues this rich Gospel teaching by reiterating an early Christian creed.

"For what I received I passed on to you as of first importance: that Christ died for our sins according to the Scriptures, that he was buried, that he was raised on the third day according

to the Scriptures, and that he appeared to Cephas, and then to the Twelve. After that, he appeared to more than five hundred of the brothers and sisters at the same time, most of whom are still living, though some have fallen asleep. Then he appeared to James, then to all the apostles, and last of all he appeared to me also, as to one abnormally born." (1 Corinthians 15:3-8)

2. **Love-saturated.** Simply put, those folks in Acts liked to hang out. The Greek word for fellowship is "koinonia." This rich fellowship is a visible display of participation, sharing, and partnership. They didn't just go to church; they were the church. They lived out their faith every day and with each other. The Acts 2 church wasn't about a building but instead about building a body of believers who changed and moved the world. Pastor Alistair Begg has said, "We do not need a church that will move with the world. We don't need a church that will accommodate itself to every passing fancy. We need a church that will move the world." Amen! Yessssss.

Love can do that. Jesus' love through us can do that.

3. **Christ-Centered.** When the early church met, they broke bread. Most scholars believe this is more than eating. Many believe this is also partaking of the sacrament of communion. The early Christians did this on the

first day of the week (Acts 20:7). At the center of their teaching was a resurrected Jesus. At the center of their lives was Jesus. At the center of their meetings was Jesus. Communion kept (and keeps) the work of Jesus in the forefront of minds. Christ's blood (wine/juice) and body (bread) represent the finished salvation work of Jesus on the cross. Additionally, and by faith, Communion ingested represents a resurrected Jesus living in us now (Galatians 2:20). We are not left to our own devices.

4. **God-connected.** How do we connect with God? Prayer, worship, and the Word of God are powerful ways to do so. Talking to God (prayer), ascribing worth and value to God (worship), and God talking to us (the Word) connects us to Him. Telling God our hearts, giving God our hearts, and listening to God's heart constitutes an excellent path for God-connection.

The first church in Acts depended upon God. God was their source, and they needed to be plugged in. Prayer and the Word were vital. The leaders of the church knew this. There were logistical issues to handle when the Acts 2 church grew from 3,000 to 5,000 by Acts chapter 6. The prominent leaders decided they would appoint other capable people to do the work of ministry and handle the problems at hand SO THAT the leaders could stick to their priority of prayer and the Word. Because of such discipline and leadership priorities, Jesus' church multiplied, and the Gospel was spread. How cool is that?

How crazy is that? Four elements seem to be the glue for the New Testament church. The Western, modern church has scrambled, gambled, and fumbled to figure out how things should work. All along, there were four pistons tucked away in the pages of scripture and ready to be revved up. It's as if an old classic car with a smokin' engine had been stashed away under a dusty canvas in a country barn.

Let's pull the canvas off. Let's crank this up. Let's rev God's engine and watch what He does.

At Lifebridge, we communicate those same Acts 2 pistons this way: Love. Feed. Spur. Connect.

We...

Love people one at a time (love-saturated).

Feed people the Word of God (Bible-based).

Spur people to serve (love-saturated).

Connect people to God through prayer and worship (Christ-centered / God-connected).

Love, feed, spur, connect. Love, feed, spur, connect. If you keep saying it repeatedly... and maybe faster and faster, it sounds like a purring, humming engine.

God's engine.

And finally, before we roll up our sleeves, stick the key in the ignition, and crank'er up, here's an honest question to consider.

What are the pistons in the engine that drive most churches? What do most churches focus on? Many say numbers, programs, money, marketing, smoke & lights production, music, big buildings, and rock star pastors.

Do you see why many churches are in trouble?

Do you see how far we've strayed from God's design for His church?

So let's go. Love, feed, spur, connect. Are you ready to start God's engine – put the pedal to the metal and let'er roll?

Such intriguing thoughts dig up memories of an old CCM Whiteheart song, "Convertibles."[2]

Hey, are you ready to go

Got the top turned down on my GTO

Come on, let's all jump in

---

[2] Whiteheart. "Convertibles." Track 5. Don't Wait For The Movie, 1986. The Sparrow Corporation.

Gonna take this car for a little spin
Oh, hear the motor hum
Gonna ride into the endless summer sun.
Wind blowing through my hair
The sky is blue; I haven't got a care
Feels so good and free
It's just like God is sitting next to me
Oh, don't you feel it too
You gotta know that it really must be
True...

God made convertibles

The sun is shining here; you can see
It's pretty clear
God made convertibles
And this high I'm riding on is not a
Manufactured one
God made convertibles
As you put the pedal down, let Him
Lift you off the ground.

Questions

1. Read Ephesians 4:11-13. What would having "unity in the faith and in the knowledge of the Son of God" at church look like? Do you think it's possible to have a church with "the whole measure of the fullness of Christ," and what would that look like in practical terms?

2. How can the four activities/pistons mentioned in Acts 2:42 shape the identity and growth of a church?

3. Of the four pistons, which one comes easy for you, and which is harder? Why is that?

4. How have you seen churches try to grow and fail based on their own efforts and ingenuity? What excites you about employing the four pistons?

Notes

CHAPTER ONE

Love People One At A Time

Church growth gurus believe that a new person entering a church will decide within the first five minutes if they will come back for a second look. This means the parking team has a bigger job than just parking cars.

Pastors watch closely how new people enter an auditorium and look around inquisitively. Most pastors wonder if the new person wants excitement, vitality, and a growing, dynamic place.

Conversely, most new people are looking for love. While many church leaders focus on crowds, most people ask if anyone will see them… as individuals and not just a part of the crowd. People desperately need to feel loved.

When someone goes through the awkward and often strange exercise of checking out a church, they are looking for two things: God and love.

A social-media-drenched population has a thirst for interaction. Will a church see someone as a valued individual beyond a heart emoji and a "like?"

This is a serious mandate for current church members to stop looking for a place to sit and find someone to love. As much as pastors and leaders fret about the size of their church, most unchurched and new folks coming through the doors don't care about such hyped nonsense. The work is figuring out how to love people one at a time.

Loving people one at a time is the first piston of God's engine for His church.

These days, big ideas of belonging abound. Have you wondered why a fickle sport like pickleball has taken off like a rocket? Belonging. People have an acute desire to belong to anything and everything. Much of the LGBTQ community is driven by this exact need.

However, in the modern Western church, even the people inside – the attendees and members, do not feel a keen sense of belonging. And so this must be said: Membership is NOT the goal. Belongership is. (And yes, we have a patent on that word!)

Several years back, Thomas Rainer wrote a book, "Surprising Insights of the Unchurched."[3] In his study, Rainer discovered that unchurched and de-churched people aren't looking for a loving church but one that personally loves them.

Somewhat infamously, a church in Ohio printed in their Sunday bulletin for years: "The end of your search for a friendly church."

But they weren't.

Beyond the pride worn by the church's members for such a great slogan, the people were relatively inbred and uncaring for each other – let alone for a visitor or lost person.

Rainer uncovered his unchurched surprises when the seeker-targeted movement was in full swing. This way of doing church was championed by a mega-church called Willow Creek in Barrington, Illinois. Willow had asked people what it would take to get them to church. The surveyed answers included great music, lights, production, drama, a non-churchy atmosphere, and casual attire. With collected data, Willow Creek built one of the first seeker-targeted churches and grew by the thousands.

---

3 Rainer, Thomas. Surprising Insights of the Unchurched. Zondervan, Grand Rapids, MI (2001).

However, thirty years into their spiritual experiment, Willow admitted through a revealing study of their church members that few were centered on Christ. Willow's study, "Reveal," proved their efforts fell short and highlighted their gathering of consumers rather than those who had surrendered to Jesus.

Rainer's study was different from Willow's original survey. Rainer's team talked with spiritual seekers who ended up going to church. What brought you to the church—or back to the church? The answers were stunning: truth, the Bible, prayer, worship, and love. A church that personally loved them was able to attract and keep them.

At Lifebridge, we ask this: How valued do people feel after visiting our church?

Christian parents of college-age kids want their kids to connect with a church when they go off to the far country and begin their life journey. When a first-year college student walks into a new church in a new city, the parents want their child loved well.

If, after his first church visit, the freshman calls home and says, "Mom & Dad... I didn't like that church at all. Nobody spoke to me. I sat alone and couldn't wait to get out the doors. Nobody seemed to care that I was even there and that I wanted to find a great new church!" If that was your kid, wouldn't you want to call up the pastor of that loser church and give him an angry piece of your mind – in Jesus' name!?

But...

Suppose your college freshman phoned home after visiting a new church and said, "Mom and Dad... wow. I went to a great church. An older dude greeted me and connected me with seven other college kids. We all sat together. The worship and teaching were great. And then... that same older greeter guy caught me afterward and asked if he and his wife could take me to lunch. They bought me a big 'ole steak at Longhorn Steak House. We exchanged names and numbers, and they said they'd look for me again next week. It was so cool."

If that were your kid, you would want to call the pastor of that church and say, "Hey, thanks for loving my kid as if he were your kid!"

The key to loving people one at a time within our church is for people to pray, "Lord, help me love this person as I would like my child to be loved."

Below is an interesting chart of the Kingdom work needed to attract and help people who belong to a church fellowship. Across the top are stages of involvement: 1) a potential guest; 2) a first-time guest; 3) a second-time guest; 4) a third-time guest; 5) an attendee with no commitment; 6) a member; 7) a Belonger (our goal!). With each category, you can also see attitudes, postures, and questions on their minds.

Notice the retention rate categories. It goes up with each of the three first visits. However, the retention rate drops if someone slips into merely attending. Incredibly interesting is that a person who goes through some formalized membership has a retention rate of 50%. Why is that? If someone becomes a member and doesn't plug in, there is a 50/50 chance they'll stay.

Look at that retention rate when someone becomes a Belonger. Wow.

From Potential Guest To Belonger

The Stages of Engagement	Potential Guest	1st-Time Guest	2nd-Time Guest	3rd-Time Guest	Attend / No Commit	Member	Belonger
Retention Rate	-	25%	50%	75%	10%	50%	50-75%
Basic Attitude and Posture	I'm open to an invitation	I'm checking you out	I'm open and interested	I'm here if you want me	I'm ready to grow & help	I'm ready to belong	I'm important and I belong here
Questions On Their Minds	Does it sound enjoyable or threatening? Will I be pressured? Will my friends be there?	Am I comfortable? Did I enjoy it? Did it meet my needs? Am I going to return?	Do I fit in? Will anyone remember me?	Do you really want me? Get to know me! Plug me in. Help me feel needed.	How can I help? How do I study the Bible? Are group study classes available?	What is my financial and time commitment? What is our mission? What is God's purpose and will for me?	Will I be a good leader? What if I fail? How do I know my contribution adds value? How do I keep growing and serving?

Adapted from "Winning the Backdoor War" by Jonathan Gainsburgh

The Biblical Solution

Luke 15 is about lost things—sheep, coins, and a son. In particular, this chapter is about you, me, and all lost people. Jesus has a vast, incredible heart for people disconnected and far away from Him. His passion was on full display, and religious leaders who didn't care as much for people as they did their laws mumbled and grumbled against Jesus' compassion.

In Luke 15:1-7, there is one lost sheep and ninety-nine in the pen. Almost one hundred people are inside the church, but one lost person is outside. What the Good Shepherd (representative of Jesus) does is irrational. This is poor business-like behavior. However, this parable should make you feel incredibly loved because Jesus leaves the ninety-nine to find and love you.

Just you.

Wow.

Then, in verses 8-10 of Luke 15, a poor woman has ten coins but loses one. There's a frantic search in her first-century, one-bedroom house. The dirt floors make efforts tenuous. The loss of one coin makes budgeting almost impossible. The frantic search pays off, and the lost coin is found. Neighbors and friends are messaged; there is a flurry within the group text, complete with emojis, memes, and exclamation points.

God searches, and angels party when the rescue is complete.

That one lost coin was/is you.

One hundred sheep.

Ten coins.

One lost son in Luke 15:11-32.

Like the sheep and coins, the lost son is about you.

Jesus loved YOU one at a time and celebrated when you came home. He wants us to love people the same way... one at a time so they will come home, too.

Beyond Jesus' parable about lost sheep, coins, and sons, Jesus modeled how to love people one at a time.

Flip a few chapters to the right of Luke 15, and check out what's happening in Luke 19.

You may remember the character in this story, who is set in a town called Jericho. There was a short, stubby little man. He was a wee little man, and a wee little man was he. What kind of tree did he climb? A Sycamore tree – for the Lord he wanted to see. You may have learned that very well from Vacation Bible School. You may not have learned the incredible nuances of this remarkable story.

Zacchaeus was a horrible chief tax collector. He worked for Rome and extorted his people. Zacchaeus collected tax money for Rome but then cheated his fellow Jewish neighbors out of more money to line his fat pockets.

Zacchaeus had the authority to tax people on anything and everything. You've got four wheels on your wagon? There would be ridiculous taxes for each wheel. How many chickens do you have? More tax money. You're a rather large person, and you suck in more oxygen than most. That's going to be an added tax. You get the picture of what's going on.

What did the people of Jericho think of Zacchaeus? By the way, his name in Hebrew meant "Pure One." Did anybody ever call Zacchaeus "Pure One?" Did anyone ever call Zacchaeus by the name his mother and father gave him? It's doubtful anyone engaged and talked with Zacchaeus beyond an argument – let alone call him by name.

In Luke 19:1-10, Jesus moves beyond the ogling crowd. He goes straight to the bottom of a fateful tree. Zacchaeus is perched in its branches. The very first thing Jesus says is…

Zacchaeus.

Pure One.

Jesus calls this ornery cuss by his name. When was the last time Zacchaeus heard "Zacchaeus?" How frequently (or infrequently) do people hear their names in our fast-paced world?

And then, Jesus has lunch with "the pure one."

It's the power of a shared meal.

Jesus loved Zacchaeus one person at a time.

The story ends with Zacchaeus repenting and changing his life. He was saved because he was loved very well... one person at a time.

Our challenge as believers is to pray, "Lord, show me a Zacchaeus to love well today."

Throughout the Gospels, we see Jesus teaching crowds but loving individuals. You can lead a crowd, but it's tough to love a crowd. When Jesus healed, he laid his hands *on each one* (Luke 4:38-40).

Have you been to the doctor lately? The average time spent with a patient is 3.5 minutes. Did the doctor look you in the eye? Did he stroll into the ice-cold shame chamber, roll up to the computer screen, ask questions with his back turned, and then claim the nurse would be right in with your prescription? Hopefully, you were helped and healed, but did you feel valued... important... loved?

Jesus loved people one at a time, even when hanging on a cruel cross. He expressed compassion and concern for his family. He asked God to forgive people and told one desperate man hanging next to him that they would be in paradise together. Even in excruciating pain, Jesus was driven to love well—one at a time.

Let's Get Practical

How can a local church mobilize its members and leaders to love people one at a time? And here's a critical insight: When we love people one at a time, they add up after a while. The church grows!

As leaders and family of Lifebridge, we want to interact with new people intentionally. Sometimes, the 5-minute rule needs to be applied. Don't talk to people you know for the first five minutes after the service! We can quickly get comfortable with who we know and miss those we don't.

We want to memorize names. You will memorize what's important. People we love one at a time are important. To help with this, on Sundays, we give name tags to everyone – not just bright red ones that flash "VISITOR" to our guests.

We hope everyone at Lifebridge will see themselves as a greeter, not just the Greeter Team working the doors on Sunday.

We ask pastors, staff, and leaders to mingle with people before and after services. We know we can't love people one at a time when leaders are stuck in their offices or sipping on bottled water in the green room. (We don't have a green room!)

We ask each ministry area to organize in ways that will love people one at a time. We know this will mean different things for our Children's Ministry, Student Ministry, Worship Ministry, Singles Ministry, Men's and Women's Ministry, and others.

We intentionally focus on individuals rather than large numbers. In the Bible, numbers are essential. There's an entire Old Testament book devoted to numbers! However, you'll be hard-pressed to see posted or printed attendance numbers. We track attendance but work to avoid letting that be a trap and pursued goal.

As we work on loving people one at a time, we also try to love our staff one at a time. This necessitates our encouraging and developing new volunteer leaders. How does this help our staff? Using more of the body of Christ helps the staff to avoid burnout.

This helps us with staff retention and can even create healthier marriages and families for the staff we love.

This kind of thinking is also a great leadership development tool. Our practical philosophy helps motivate current staff and leaders to develop future leaders. For future leaders to develop, current leaders must get out of the way more.

Many churches fail to develop and mobilize leaders because current leaders and staff think they are too important.

Do you see how such an approach to leadership helps us love our staff and future leaders one at a time?

Additionally, as we love people one at a time, we are committed to following up exhaustively.

The story is told about the top-grossing Domino's Pizza store in America. Where was that store located? New York? Nope. Los Angeles? Nope. Atlanta? Nice try, but nope. Strangely, there was a year when the top-grossing Domino Pizza store was in Des Moines, Iowa. Yup. Crazy, huh? How did they achieve this unbelievable accomplishment?

They followed up exhaustively. When someone ordered a pizza on Monday, that same family received a phone call Tuesday night asking how their pizza was. Who does that? The top-grossing Domino Pizza store does. Little leaguers were at their house when the family got their day-after-pizza follow-up call. Because Dominos reached out, the dad ordered more pizza for the starving sandlot sluggers— story after such stories unfolded because of the caring hearts that followed up.

Lifebridge asks new people to fill out a connection or response card when they are ready to do so. In exchange, we give out first-time guest gift bags. We are also liberal with appropriate guest emails and phone calls and will grab a meal together if possible. Other gifts offered to new guests are Bibles and a once-a-quarter Newcomer's Lunch, complete with a free meal and face-time with staff and elders.

These are just a few ways we try to love people one at a time on Sundays at Lifebridge.

How You Can Love People One At A Time

Indeed, you can help us on Sundays and as a church to love well.

But have you ever considered how you can love people one at a time beyond Sunday at church?

You can map your neighborhood. Start slow and small. Who lives in the houses beside you, behind you, and across the street? Do you know their names? If you have their names, start praying for them.

Plan a time when you can meet and eat together. You could invite all the families you have mapped to a BBQ or just have one family at a time over to your house for a meal. Special occasions are also incredibly designed for getting together and eating. Always eat! Halloween gatherings, post-Thanksgiving meals to feast on leftovers, Christmas parties, 4th of July BBQs, Memorial or Labor Day relaxed weekends, and the Superbowl are great times to hang out and eat. Always eat. Eating together uses the universal language of love to anyone across the table.

What happens if they accept your dinner invitation? Yikes!

Just listen.

Ask questions.

Find out their story.

Most everyone likes to tell their story. Find out if there are any ways you could help them or serve them. Do their kids need rides? Could you watch their kids play sports, band concerts, or plays? Is anyone sick? Could you help with meals or mowing the lawn? A neighbor is doing a DIY deck overhaul, and you could lend a helping hand. Be creative, open, and ready.

Initially, you should go slow with a church invite. Trust in God's timing. You don't have to preach or prove your theology. If you connect and love your neighbors one at a time, there will be a time… God's time… when you can share some of your Jesus story and maybe invite them to church.

But here is the constant pushback to loving people: When do I ever have the time and energy for one more relationship – let alone six or seven?

In their book, The Art of Neighboring, Jay Pathak and Dave Runyon suggest, "We live in a world that values production, results, and activity. Today, we have more time-saving devices at our disposal than any generation in the history of the world, yet we feel as though we have less and less time to get things done. We live our lives at warp speed. We believe lies like this: Things will settle down someday. More will be enough someday. Everybody lives like this.

The healthiest person who ever lived was Jesus. He got a lot done, but hurriedness never comes to mind when we read about his life. Jesus came to offer us a different way of living. (Matthew 11:28-30)

The decision boils down to the need to figure out what is more important and then live by that decision.

This may mean God will call you to say no to some good things so you can focus on the really important things. We must learn how to keep the main thing the main thing. If we don't, choices will be made for us. In essence, we just let life happen passively. Time spent surfing the internet, playing video games, or just watching reruns of our favorite sitcoms won't amount to anything of value.

We must stop making life about what's only convenient to us and our often self-serving ways.

Being a good neighbor is an art, not a science.

Do you live at a pace that allows you to be available to those around you? And if not, are all of the things I'm doing more important than taking the Great Commandment literally?"[4]

"Love the Lord your God with all your heart and with all your soul and with all your mind and with all your strength.' The second is this: 'Love your neighbor as yourself.'[c] There is no commandment greater than these." (Mark 12:30-31)

Love God and people, one at a time.

---

[4] Pathak & Runyon, The Art of Neighboring, Baker Books, Grand Rapids, MI (2012), pgs. 44-47.

Questions

1. Read through Luke 15. What are the commonalities and differences in the three stories? Reflect on a time when you felt lost or separated from God. What steps did you take to reconnect with Him, and how can you support others in their journey to find their way back to God? Consider the father's reaction in the parable of the prodigal son. How can we emulate his grace and forgiveness in our relationships, especially towards those who may have wronged us or strayed from the path?

2. Describe one or two people who have influenced your life.

3. Why do some churches focus more on numbers rather than individuals?

4. Can you recall an instance in a church setting in which you personally were loved one at a time?

5. Why do some smaller churches - though the members think they are loving- feel unloving to visitors and new attendees?

6. What's one practical thing you can do to apply "loving people one at a time" in your life and at Lifebridge?

Notes

CHAPTER TWO

Feed People The Word of God

Growing up, many sang an old hymn called "Power In The Blood." During week-long revivals, song evangelists (the song leader) would pump up the crowd and see how many "powers" they could sing during the chorus. You would have to sing very fast, but you could get a lot of "powers" in one measure of beats and music.

Every church you pass on your way to church wants more power, and they've sped things up considerably with hyperactivity to get a lot of "powers" in.

The power of teaching the Bible thoroughly forms piston number two of God's engine: Feed people the Word of God.

However, our culture is Biblically illiterate. While 50% of the U.S. population is said to be functionally illiterate, Biblical literacy is most definitely at an all-time low.

During World War II, British troops were trapped on the beach of Dunkirk off the coast of France. As the Germans were bearing down on the fearful Brits, a veiled communication was sent to the English homeland. The message was simple: "And if not."[5]

What was that about?

Do you know what they were trying to articulate to friends, family, and fellow citizens who knew of their pending doom?

People in the 1940s knew precisely what it meant. They also knew their Bibles. "And if not," comes from an incredible story in the Old Testament book of Daniel. In chapter three, Shadrach, Meshach, and Abednego are held as young immigrants forced to bow to King Nebuchadnezzar.

Three teenage dissidents refused to bow and conveyed to King Nebuchadnezzar their belief in a God who would save them from a fiery furnace. "And if not," Shadrach, Meshach, and Abednego would still not bow to anyone but their living God.

---

5   https://www.christianitytoday.com/2001/08/reversing-biblical-memory-loss/

The British troops wanted folks back in Great Britain to know they believed God would spare them. "And if not," they still would not bow nor give in to Germany and Hitler. Such strong communication was given and understood because the power of God's Word was alive and well.

Today, many of our churches are fast becoming Biblically illiterate. Evangelical worship services seem to be using the Bible less and less. At the same time, people are smart and know the difference between hearing human words and God's Word.

People leaving a church gathering will either say, "Pastor, that was a great story you told..." or "I heard God say..." Barna suggests nearly 70% of American churchgoers rarely experience God when they go to church.[6]

Thomas Rainer documents how unchurched folks aren't looking for entertaining churches but Biblically deep and challenging ones.

At Lifebridge, ask questions like: After involvement in our church, how well will each person know and love the Bible? Will the members of our church have a solid Biblical foundation for their future? How much of the Bible are they getting? If people gave Lifebridge four years of their lives, could we give them the entire Bible?

---

6   https://www.barna.com/research/current-perceptions/

The Biblical Solution

Hebrews 4:12 says, "For the word of God is alive and active. Sharper than any double-edged sword, it penetrates even to dividing soul and spirit, joints and marrow; it judges the thoughts and attitudes of the heart."

The Bible is living. It's alive! This means God is a God who speaks. If you're looking for a word from God, read His Word. God still speaks through His Word and Spirit; the two will never contradict. God will not convince you there are many ways to heaven when the Bible says there is only one (John 14:6). God will never lead you to exasperate your kids nor disrespect your parents (Ephesians 6:1-4). The Cubs will never be better than the Atlanta Braves.

OK. That last biased item is not in the Bible, but you get the point.

The Word of God is also active; it has the power to effect its own results. The Bible is self-installing.

Do you remember the dark, dark days of DOS computer programming? It took a computer engineer to install a simple program. Today, a window pops up and says, "Install Now?" All you do is click and go. Programs, links, and add-ons are all self-installing.

With the Bible, you just read it, and it's self-installing. We believe reading the Bible aloud in a worship service is enormously beneficial.

Have you experienced a preacher who is long with words and short on application? You sat through his rant – now you're haaangry and ready to hit Cracker Barrel. But wait... an invitation offered for people to come forward with spiritual decisions unfolds before your weary eyes. Indeed, this will be quick, right?

Nope.

A flood of people went forward and cried out to Jesus at the altar.

What just happened? The preacher was dry and lifeless. But... he used a lot of scripture. What he did right was use the Word of God. He fed people the Word of God, and the Bible self-installed. Amazing.

The Bible is extraordinary. It's a flashlight for our often hidden path (Psalms 119:105). The Word of God never sits and does nothing; it will not return void (Isaiah 55:11). All scripture is God-breathed (II Timothy 3:16); it's how God speaks to us and is what He wants us to know.

II Timothy 4:1-2 reads: "In the presence of God and of Christ Jesus, who will judge the living and the dead, and in view of his appearing and his kingdom, I give you this charge: Preach the word; be prepared in season and out of season; correct, rebuke and encourage—with great patience and careful instruction."

We are given a clarion call to preach the Word. The command is to preach and declare the Gospel boldly – not merely to discuss, post memes about, study, or banter in coffee shops. Preach the Word! God's Word changes lives, not our human words about God's Word. D.L. Moody was a much-loved preacher who said, "The Bible was not given to increase our knowledge, but to change our lives."[7]

Let's Get Practical

What are the ways we feed people the Word of God? First, we give away free Bibles to anyone who needs one. This is an excellent use of our money!

We will often threaten to take Bible verses off our screens. Why would we do that?

We want people to carry and dig into a Bible and not rely on a lifeless video screen. We often talk about having a legacy Bible.

---

[7] https://www.navigators.org/blog/the-bible-was-not-given-to-increase-our-knowledge/#:~:text=This%20quote%2C%20often%20attributed%20to%20the%20American%20evangelist,apply%20it%20in%20order%20to%20know%20God%20Himself.

Many family members will ask about a left-behind Bible when a loved one passes. Did they have one? What was written, circled, and noted within the pages? When a legacy Bible is passed down, it's an exceptional, personal, powerful thing.

We encourage actual Bibles to write in, circle words and ideas, and make notes of how God directs. Many may use cell phones or digital notepads as a Bible, but nothing beats the real deal.

During worship services, we will use the Bible in our music. We'll also display scripture on our video screens during musical interludes. We work incredibly hard to sing the Gospel, theology, and Biblically rich lyrics.

Sometimes, we use scripture to create media, dramas, and videos. We'll stand and formally read the central text of the day's message. We typically respond after reading God's Word with the reader saying, "This is the Word of the Lord," and the congregation responds, "Thanks be to God." This is not meant to be dry, repetitive religious practice as much as it holds up the Word of God as an absolute authority in our lives and church.

We pray specific Biblical texts over the congregation. We'll most likely preach expository messages that dig into one central passage of scripture. The Bible will be the heart of the message. We also like to teach through the complete books of the Bible. In doing so, we believe all the other relevant topics will be covered within God's living and active Word.

Additionally, we promote Lifegroups (small groups) where people can discuss a sermon and God's Word further. Sermon outlines and Lifegroup questions are posted weekly on various apps and digital platforms.

Finally, here is a crucial insight: God did a great job on the Bible. We should use it! As sheep, our Good Shepherd leads us with the rod of his Word.

Do you know when sheep get into trouble? It's when they wander off from the herd as they move head-down and eat from tuft of grass to tuft of grass. Once a sheep is alone, they become afraid. They often can stop eating. Alone, scared, and hungry, a lost sheep is susceptible to wolves or rocky hills where they can fall.

Did you know a sheep can fall on its back and not be able to turn over? It can die that way. Geesh. And the Bible compares us to sheep— Ding dang!

Sheep that are alone, hungry, fearful, and susceptible can quickly become unhealthy.

And when sheep are unhealthy, reproduction is the first biological function to go south. Unhealthy sheep do not reproduce.

Well-fed sheep are healthy, joy-filled, and reproductive. Sheep close to the shepherd listen to the shepherd. They eat well. They're happy, and they reproduce. We hope the sheep at Lifebridge are well-fed through the Word of God. The engine of God's church hums and purrs when we feed people the Word of God.

What Can You Do To Feed People The Word Of God?

Start with grabbing a free Bible at church or purchasing one for yourself. We recommend a NIV or ESV translation. As discussed previously, use your Bible as a legacy Bible that will last and be passed down to kids and grandkids.

Set aside daily relational time with God. Sit quietly and read His Word. You may want to start with the book of John. You may want to start with a Bible reading plan like the McCheyne plan. There are many apps and digital platforms that can be helpful. The Bible Project videos can be incredibly insightful as a guide. A translation like Eugene Peterson's "The Message Bible" can offer practical, street-level help as you dive into God's Word.

You can read a passage of scripture using the A.C.T.S. acronym. In the text, is there something to:

A - adore God about?

C - confess a sin to God?

T - thank God?

S - Supplication... pray something on behalf of someone else?

You could try Pastor Rick Warren's SPACEPETS acronym as you camp out on a particular passage within the Bible.

Is there a:

S - **Sin** to confess? Do I need to make any restitution?

P - **Promise** to claim? Is it a universal promise? Have I met the condition(s)?

A - **Attitude** to change? Am I willing to work on a negative attitude and begin building toward a positive one?

C - **Command** to obey? Am I willing to do it no matter how I feel?

E - **Example** to follow? Is it a positive example for me to copy or a negative one to avoid?

P - **Prayer** to pray? Is there anything I need to pray back to God?

E - **Error** to avoid? Is there any problem that I should be alert to or aware of?

T - **Truth** to believe? What new things can I learn about God the Father, Jesus Christ, the Holy Spirit, or other Biblical teachings?

S - **Something** to praise God for? Is there something here I can be thankful for?[8]

Feed yourself first before taking on the challenge of feeding others.

But when you are ready, think about a weekly time of devotions (prayer and the Word) with your spouse and family. Make this a fun time and not legalistic. Remember, our time in God's Word helps us relationally with Him. We must guard ourselves from turning time in God's Word into something religious that can check a churchy box.

Keep a living, active journal next to your living and active Word. Are there thoughts, ideas, and obedience items you could write down due to spending time with God and His incredible Word?

Join a Lifegroup (small group) where you can discuss The Word with other believers.

Sign up for a class at Lifebridge that will strengthen your Bible knowledge while addressing relevant life issues. We recommend you start with our Jesus 101 class that addresses foundational doctrines like the cross, sin, baptism, confession, repentance, communion, and Jesus!

---

8   https://www.joshhunt.com/2019/05/01/s-p-a-c-e-p-e-t-s/

Do an annual assessment of your love and hunger for God's Word. Notice we didn't encourage you to assess how much you read the Bible. Such thinking can become heavy, overwhelming, and religious.

John Ortberg said, "The goal is not for us to get through the Scriptures. The goal is to get the Scriptures through us."[9]

How much is your legacy Bible marked and used compared to one year ago? What's been highlighted that wasn't last year?

Do verses and Biblical principles come to the forefront of your thinking as you counsel others? Are others coming to you more and more for counsel?

Is scripture being recalled and coming up in conversations or prayers? Memorizing verses is such a great discipline for this. Put 3x5 cards of critical verses on your bathroom mirror, car visor, or office desk. How many verses can you memorize in a week?

The Good Shepherd wants you well-fed with The Word. As a result of Bible exposure, healthy sheep will be joy-filled and reproductive – you can feed people the Word of God. How cool is that?

---

9   https://libquotes.com/john-ortberg/quote/lbh6g9d

Questions

1. Read Hebrews 4:12. How have you experienced the word of God being "alive and active" in your life? What does it mean to you that God's word is "sharper than any double-edged sword"? In what ways can we allow God's word to judge the thoughts and attitudes of our hearts?

2. Read 2 Timothy 4:1-2. How do you interpret Paul's exhortation to "preach the word" in today's context? Why do you think it's essential to be "prepared in season and out of season"? How can we balance correcting, rebuking, and encouraging others with "great patience and careful instruction"?

3. Why do you think reading Biblical texts in worship services has declined in modern churches?

4. If God were to grade your Biblical knowledge, what grade would you receive? After a few years at Lifebridge, how well should people know the Bible?

5. On a scale of 1-10 (10 being great), how important would people attending our church believe the Bible is as a part of the church service?

6. What is one practical thing you can do to improve having the Bible more in your life?

Notes

CHAPTER THREE

Spur People To Serve

Power is a necessary and sometimes tenuous thing. Thanks to state and Federal tax exemptions, people in Georgia were given great deals to lease all-electric Nissan Leafs for two years. This led to a surge in the number of Leafs on the roads and made driving practically free for many Georgians. With a full charge, Leaf drivers had 100 miles to play with. However, the original Leaf's charge meter counted down the miles, making it a game to conserve power with every mile driven, punch of the gas pedal, notch more on the heater, or volume increase on the radio.

The screen went blank once the charge was drained to seven miles, causing panic. Leaf owners were fearfully trained to get to a charging station quickly! Unfortunately, some Nissans were driven to zero and were abandoned alongside the road. What do you do with an electric vehicle that's out of power? In the early days of all-electric cars, a tow was the only solution to poorly managed power.

There is also power in the church we want to tap into and not drain at Lifebridge.

It's the power of living and loving like Jesus that spurs people to serve. So many people go to church; we want to BE the Church.

Francis Schaeffer wrote, "If we do not show beauty in the way we treat each other, then in the eyes of the world and in the eyes of our own children, we are destroying the truth we proclaim."[10] How will we serve and show beauty, starting with each other and then the world?

In many churches, Christians view worship attendance as essential, but evangelism or serving as somewhat optional. Could this be why churches in America fail to grow significantly from year to year? Why do so many churches struggle with an ongoing lack of volunteers? Those who do volunteer are often overworked and burned out.

Interestingly, people looking for a church aren't looking for a church to hide in and do nothing. Most people want to find a place (church) where they can serve and make a real difference in our world.

---

10 Francis A. Schaeffer, 2 Contents, 2 Realities (Downers Grove, 1975), pages 1-32.

We like to ask this fundamental question: After becoming involved at Lifebridge, how motivated will people be to pray for, serve, and love others into the Kingdom of Jesus? How motivated will people be to reach out and serve their community with love?

Pastor Rick Warren claims, "Faithful servants never retire. You can retire from your career, but you will never retire from serving God."[11] How does that mini-sermon make you feel? Tired? Energized?

The Biblical Solution

Take a look at John 1:41-45. What do you see? What's going on within this passage?

"The first thing Andrew did was to find his brother Simon and tell him, "We have found the Messiah" (that is, the Christ). And he brought him to Jesus. Jesus looked at him and said, "You are Simon, son of John. You will be called Cephas" (which, when translated, is Peter). The next day, Jesus decided to leave for Galilee. Finding Philip, he said to him, "Follow me." Philip, like Andrew and Peter, was from the town of Bethsaida. Philip found Nathanael and told him, "We have found the one Moses wrote about in the Law, and

---

11 Warren, Rick. The Purpose Driven Life, Zondervan, Grand Rapids, MI (2002). Pg. 262.

about whom the prophets also wrote—Jesus of Nazareth, the son of Joseph."

How did both Simon Peter and Nathanael come to meet Jesus? It's pretty simple. They were brought to Jesus by friends who served them. How did you come to Jesus? How did you find your way to Lifebridge? Odds are you were served in such a way that you took a step forward. Somebody at some time assisted you and helped you on your way to Jesus and His Church.

Do you remember the story of a woman Jesus encountered at a well? Jesus asked her for a drink of water, and she obliged. After an intriguing conversation, Jesus told her details about her broken life. The woman was amazed and knew she was speaking with a prophet. Jesus offered living water that quenched thirst well beyond a Gatorade. Jesus reveals He's more than a prophet; He's the long-awaited Messiah. The woman is blown away that the Messiah would stop and talk to a lowly, shamed, and discarded Samaritan woman. Immediately, this changed woman ran into her town, where most people had learned to ignore the wild rants of such a sinful woman. And then we see this in John 4:39-42:

"Many of the Samaritans from that town believed in him because of the woman's testimony, "He told me everything I ever did." So when the Samaritans came to him, they urged him to stay with them, and he stayed two days. And because of his words, many more became believers. They said to the woman, "We no longer believe

just because of what you said; now we have heard for ourselves, and we know that this man really is the Savior of the world."

Why did this Samaritan village suddenly believe in Jesus? It was because of the woman's testimony. She served her people with the incredible story of the redemption and restoration of Jesus – the Messiah. She was spurred to serve the other Samaritans by discussing Jesus with them.

In John 6:38-40, Jesus says these power-packed words:

"For I have come down from heaven not to do my will but to do the will of him who sent me. And this is the will of him who sent me, that I shall lose none of all those he has given me, but raise them up at the last day. For my Father's will is that everyone who looks to the Son and believes in him shall have eternal life, and I will raise them up at the last day."

Simply stated, Jesus' will was to do the will of His Father in heaven. This is called "the power of congruence in mission." Jesus wanted to do what God wanted to do, and vice versa. Jesus' earthly mission accomplished a heavenly mission.

Let's Get Practical

How do we mobilize the army that IS the church at Lifebridge? (Remember, we're still loving people one at a time.) The problem is not a matter of resources. Churches aren't equipping the resources—they're all dammed up! If you followed that, you understand our resources are people, and we're just not using them well.

The strategy is to figure out the exponential impact. That may sound slippery and "church-growthy," but allow us the space and math to explain.

Let's say you start a community impact project with 50 people. The idea is for each person to influence one other person per year. Let's do the math...

You would have 100 people at the end of one year. Did you follow that? At the end of year two, you would have 200 people. Are you still with us?

At the end of year three, 400 people will be impacted.

At the end of year five, 1,600.

At this point, our exercise becomes increasingly more complicated for math-challenged people.

How many people would you have at the end of year five?

51,200.

Let's jump ahead to year fifteen. What do you think? Does your head hurt yet? 1.6 million people. Dang.

By the end of year twenty, 52 million people are impacted.

And after twenty-five years of one person impacting one person per year, you would end up with 1.6 billion people influenced.

How cool is that? THAT is exponential impact. THAT is how you impact the world for Jesus!

The point is this: if we have 50 people in our church, we have an army!

At one point in their marketing history, Blue Diamond Almond growers had this awesome slogan: "One can a week – that's all we ask!" That's the potential of exponential sales garnering exponential growth.

At Lifebridge, we believe our people must be intentionally trained to love and serve others. We don't assume loving and serving will magically happen. Our broken, human default is to be served, and many churches train people in that same manner (great coffee, comfortable atmosphere, care for your kids, great music, practical messages, and we'll change your car's oil while you worship!).

We've found that when believers pray regularly for their friends, God softens their friends' hearts and opens opportunities for love and service.

How exactly do we attempt to mobilize our army?

We ask and train Lifebridge members to pray for their friends who don't know Jesus. We ask people to create prayer requests for those people by writing them on our response cards and turning them in.

We ask people to pray for and serve their friends and community through church invites, Lifegroups (small groups), special events, BBQs, and anything and everything! As we do life, we want people to pray for others and serve. As we go about our days, we hope to have the mind of Christ towards others.

We will celebrate baptisms and tell stories often. We offer message series invitation cards to give to a friend, co-worker, neighbor, or Publix check-out person.

We offer, from time to time, classes to train people how to share their faith.

We create serving opportunities with our Men's and Women's ministries and corporate events to serve and connect with people. Occasionally, we dismiss our gatherings on Sunday mornings to collectively go and serve in our community.

We want people to serve people. The ultimate goal is to move people from macro to micro, where our corporate serving moves into serving initiatives in people's everyday lives. This is visible, impactful, tangible Kingdom stuff.

Spur People To Serve

In their book, "The Tangible Kingdom,"[12] Hugh Halter and Matt Smay suggests that when mission, the Gospel, and community unite, you have lasered in on Jesus' tangible Kingdom. When the Gospel compels us to love, the mission compels us to go and serve, and we are in a community of people for accountability and confidence – great, tangible Kingdom stuff happens. Check out the illustration below![13]

We aim to mobilize people through the power of a congruent mission. And we have a little secret.

---

12   Halter, Hugh, Smay, Matt. The Tangible Kingdom, Jossey-Bass, San Francisco, CA (2008).

13   https://cumc.net/test-post/

If people adopt a personal mission congruent with the church's corporate mission, they will automatically fulfill the church's mission.

Adventure Christian Church of Roseville, CA, has a mission statement: "To let God love us and love others through us."

Pretty simple stuff, right?

Adventure believes this is God's will for every believer's life. If their mission is adopted as personal, the church's corporate mission is powerfully fulfilled.

At Lifebridge, our mission can also be a personal mission. If a person loves, feeds, spurs, and connects (our 4 Pistons), our church's mission will be accomplished by default. How cool would that be?

Why wouldn't a Christian be on mission? Perhaps they are dammed up. Maybe they are stagnant rivers with no outflow. The Dead Sea is dead because it has no outflow. Adventure's Pastor, Rick Stedman, wrote, "*A mountain stream remains fresh and healthy as long as the water is allowed to flow into and through it. But if the stream becomes blocked or dammed, and water is not allowed to flow through, the stream will stagnate and become unhealthy – even poisonous. In addition, it will become full and will have no more room for additional water. In a similar way, the key to a healthy and growing Christian life is to allow God's love to flow in and through us."* [14]

So, how do we get people moving, volunteering, and serving? At Lifebridge, we want to mobilize volunteers inside our walls, knowing the outside will also be affected. Our strategy is fractals.

Do you remember 8th-grade science? A fractal is a pattern in nature that replicates itself. Some plants and crystals have similar patterns on both the macro and micro levels.

At the base or smallest point of a fern, the patterns and composition are the same as the fern grows larger. This is the idea of a fractal, and this is the key to volunteer recruitment. Some of this thinking comes from Wayne Cordeiro's book, "Doing Church As A Team."[15]

---

14 http://adventurechurch.org/aboutadventure/

15 Cordeiro, Wayne. "Doing Church as a Team: The Miracle of Teamwork and How It Transforms Churches," Bethany House, Minneapolis, MN (2001). Pgs.. 172-190.

Every volunteer is to recruit other volunteers. Fractals!

Our goal is to set up a self-replicating process. We base the volunteer recruitment process on being driven by the volunteers, not the leaders or staff. Haven't you noticed how staff and leaders can often be the bottlenecks, keeping people from plugging in and serving? Ugh.

Here's our motto:

"EVERY VOLUNTEER HAS TWO JOBS!"

Job #1: The task you volunteer for.

Job #2: To pray for and recruit others to volunteer with you, each with two jobs. Did you just see the fractal?

Think about it: What if everybody actually had two jobs? What would recruiting be like for our kid's ministry? If you started with ten people, they would become 20, then 40, then 80, then 160, then 320, then 640, and then the pastor gets up on Sunday morning and tells the church, "Hey! Quit volunteering for our kid's ministry!"

When have you ever heard a pastor say that? (smh)

And what about leadership? How does our mobilization of exponential thinking affect leadership?

How should we develop leaders and think of leadership?

Lifebridge recognizes three levels of leadership.

L1 Leadership encourages a leader to do the work of ten people

L2 Leadership tries to find ten leaders to do the work of leadership.

L3 Leadership recruits leaders who will recruit leaders. L3 leadership finds leaders who will pray for and get ten people to do the work, AND each leader recruits ten more leaders to do the same. TWO JOBS! Fractals!

And what is the result of our three levels of leadership?

L1 = Burnout. Ugh.

L2 = Limited growth and potential.

L3 = Unlimited growth, potential, and sustainability.

What Can You Do To Spur People To Serve?

In Hebrews 10, the Bible lays out great Gospel theology of what Jesus has and is doing for us. He is our high priest who has opened access to the Father with his body and blood. And then, in verse 19, there is a big "therefore."

As a result of Jesus' finished work on the cross, we should have confidence, enter into God's presence, hold on tight to hope, and agitate.

Whaaa da what? Agitate?

Yup. Incite. Provoke.

We are to spur (the Greek word, *paroxysmos,* signals agitate) each other towards love and action.

Hebrews 10:24 reads, *"And let us consider how we may **spur** one another on toward love and good deeds..."*

How do we agitate each other to serve? Perhaps we provoke and incite others by returning to the Gospel—Jesus. Jesus plus nothing = everything. It is Jesus who compels us. Do we serve to earn more of God's love and acceptance?

Nope.

We serve because we have been loved and accepted. We love and serve because Jesus first loved and served us.

When we serve, we're actually spurring and agitating others with a bit of positive Gospel peer pressure to get going—because of Jesus. We spur each other because we are Gospel-driven. Together. Here are seven spurring steps for you to consider.

Step one: Serve. Jump in. Find a need, fix a problem, and offer your expertise. Try something, even if that something changes over time. If you raise your white flag and tell someone you want to serve ... giddy up. It's game on.

Step two (and you could interchange steps one and two): Take our Spiritual Gifts 101 class to explore your unique wiring. God has created you for good works. Find God's gifts of passion, interest, and talent – and serve! In his book 'Your Devine Design," Chip Ingram states, "My joy and the impact of my life for God's Kingdom never got off the ground until I got clear on what my spiritual gifts were and then focused my time and energy on them."[16]

Step three: Fine-tune where you serve. Find a ministry inside or outside Lifebridge, and use your spiritual gifts and passion. We pray God will energize you as your gifts and passion wonderfully collide!

Step four: Don't say "yes" to too many serving ideas. People who discover their spiritual gifts and begin serving can frequently get abused at a church. At many churches, 20% of the people do 80% of the ministry work. That is unsustainable, unhealthy, and ungodly. Sometimes, people say yes to a plethora

---

[16] Ingram, Chip, Your Devine Design, Living On The Edge, Suwanee, GA (2022), pg. 30.

of agenda items, and this keeps others from areas of service. We hope to engage the entire congregation and move forward into the work of Jesus' Kingdom.

Step five: Look for a Zacchaeus. Instead of finding a seat on Sunday mornings, look for a Zacchaeus to love and serve. Remember, for good reasons, everyone ignored Zacchaeus, and nobody called him by his name. But Jesus stopped by a tree, called Zacchaeus by name, invited him to lunch, and served him. The result? Zacchaeus' life was changed and saved.

Step six: Look for opportunities to serve in all of life. When Jesus said, "Go..." he meant "as you go." As you do life, look for ways to serve. This kind of thinking includes serving at church but goes well beyond the walls of a church. You can serve a neighbor, coworker, classmate, waitress, cashier, spouse, kids, and even your jacked-up Uncle Harry at Thanksgiving—the little stuff counts.

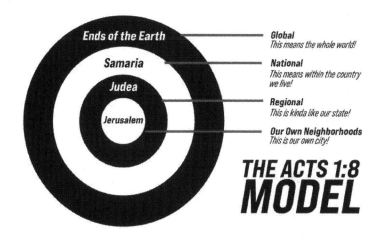

Step seven: Think of concentric circles when you think of serving. In Acts 1:8, Jesus' friends were challenged to serve in concentric circles. First in Jerusalem, then Judea, then Samaria, and then wherever in the world God may lead.

Take a look at the above illustration from Shelter Cove Community Church.[17] You may think of serving first in your church, then your city, your state, your country, and perhaps taking a mission trip somewhere in the world!

Your serving will spur others. Agitating!

Your serving may also save your marriage... your parenting... your kids.

---

17   https://sheltercovelive.com/missions/

The relentless pursuit of the great American dream has led many to believe that happiness is the goal of life and God. If you don't believe this, watch what happens to Christians, when life becomes difficult. Their faith wavers, anger towards God wells up, and depression sets in. Does this often occur because being happy is the end game?

What if God's story of creation, fall, redemption, and restoration was the goal? What if His purposes, not yours, were center stage? What if life was about a larger Kingdom than our selfish little ones?

Serving is a great way to get you out of the way. Serving is a part of God's plan to rescue you from you. Jesus ultimately rescues us, but giving our lives away like Jesus helps us find our life.

When your marriage is broken and knotted up, serve your way out. Take the spotlight off yourselves and serve others experiencing the darkness of life in greater ways than you've ever thought possible.

Bratty kids? Agitate them. Spur them to serve and see how other kids and families live in such difficulty that your kids have never dreamed of. This becomes a dynamic, life-altering wake-up call.

Serving has a great dynamic of shattering narcissistic lenses, seeing others, and grasping a God who's in control of it all.

God wants to use you. The work of Jesus spurs us – agitates us to be laborers of a greater harvest beyond any temporary stuff you're hoping to achieve.

And that happiness thing? Serving takes us higher and deeper to a joy that can stand through life's hurricanes and mountaintops. Happiness is fleeting and overrated. The joy of the Lord is what you want. Joy comes through surrender and giving your life away. Serving, spurring, and agitating is what loyal subjects of a greater Kingdom naturally want to do.

Go for it!

Questions

1. Read John 1:41-45. Who is serving whom in this passage? Can you find other New Testament stories where someone is serving another? Where do you find yourself in these stories?

2. On a scale of 1-10 (10 being excellent), how well do you serve others? How well do you see Lifebridge doing this?

3. How concerned are you that many churches focus only on themselves? Explain.

4. On a scale of 1-10 (10 being excellent), how well do you love other people? Is Lifebridge a loving church, and how would you know?

5. What is one thing you can do practically to love and serve others? What is one thing you hope Lifebridge will do or do better?

Notes

CHAPTER FOUR

Connect People To God Through Prayer And Worship

Is worship just that block of songs on Sunday mornings – for about twenty minutes, as some might think?

Uhm, no.

First and foremost, we are all worshippers. Believers and nonbelievers alike engage in acts of worship. Have you ever been to a Jason Aldean or Taylor Swift concert? The stadiums are filled with worshippers. Worship is a powerful act of ascribing worth to something or someone. It's a universal part of our human experience; we are all created to worship.

You can worship your finely manicured lawn and ascribe great worth to the new set of wheels sitting in your driveway.

Sometimes, spouses are elevated to a savior-like status. Spouses, by the way, make horrible saviors.

In the New Testament, in Romans chapter one, the writer asks if we ascribe worship to the Creator or creation. It's a challenging section of scripture.

If our eternal God was not created but created everything, how offensive would it be to focus all of our attention on creation and not the Creator? That's a huge question. Likewise, how offensive do you think it is for our all-consuming, all-giving, all-loving Creator God when we believe worship is only what happens on Sunday mornings for about twenty minutes?

And... if we're completely honest, even those twenty minutes on Sunday mornings get evaluated as to what we like, feel, and if we could "get our worship on." It seems like Sunday morning worship can also be more about the creation (us) instead of the Creator.

The Bible encourages us to become living sacrifices, which is worship. This means all of life is worship. Your marriage, shopping for bacon bits, mowing, vacationing, balancing the checkbook, voting, and hobbies are all worship. A faithful Jesus follower never steps foot outside the Kingdom of God. There is no compartmentalizing of secular and sacred. It's an all-of-life kind of thing. All of life is worship because God is the author of all life. He is worthy of the worth we ascribe to Him.

Are you getting this? Does this sound too much like Charlie Brown's teacher? "Whaaa, whaaa, whaaa, whaaa, whaaa…"

Let's simplify things: Worship is the power of a personal relationship with God.

Many pastors who graduate from Bible college face a big surprise once they leave the angel factory. After four years of daily devotions before classes, dormitory floor devotions, studying scripture, praying on dates, and praying for exams on the History of the Old Testament, Bible college grads face real-world reality. After securing their first ministry gig, ministry graduates discover how church leaders and seasoned pastors spend little time praying.

Why is this?

So many leaders tend to focus on "running the church" rather than on God, and because of how ministry is often done, God is not really needed. Can you say, "Red flag?"

Jared Wilson writes, "… pastors ought to know what the carpet in their study smells like. … the pastor should be so accustomed to being prostrate before the Lord that he can practically taste the dirt and the burnt rubber from the vacuum belt in his mouth just thinking about prayer." [18]

There are many church services today where very little time is given to prayer. Many Christians attend services regularly but can personally feel distant and disconnected from God. As stated earlier, some 70% of Americans who go to church never experience Jesus when they go. How crazy and sad is that?

The lack of prayer in believers' lives and modern evangelical churches is evidence of unacknowledged self-sufficiency and a lack of dependence upon God. The symptoms and causes of the lack of prayer are precisely parallel in the leaders' lives. We simply depend on ourselves and our own abilities rather than upon God.

Here's a poignant question for you to wrestle with. Am I (and are we) genuinely dependent upon God, or have we learned to live self-sufficient, morally upright, Christian lives? Would I notice a difference if God removed His Spirit from my life or our church? Here, in the provided white space, you can write "Dang," or "Ouch," or "Whoa."

Would you be surprised that the unchurched aren't looking for a church that only talks about God? Today, people are looking for a church where they can actually experience God.

---

18   Wilson, Jared. "Gospel Driven Ministry," Zondervan, Grand Rapids, MI (2021) pg. 51.

At Lifebridge, we believe Christians develop an intimate personal relationship with God by growing up in prayer and worship, both personally and corporately. It's essential to connect people with people (love people one at a time), but people also want desperately to connect with God.

The Biblical Solution

Knowing the busyness of religion, Jesus issued these words with some firey exhortation. *"My house was designated a house of prayer; You have made it a hangout for thieves." (Matthew 21:13)*

In Jesus' day, religion caused buying, selling, and cheating concerning animals to be used for sacrifice and worship. All of this happened within the temple—what we would call the church. The worship got lost, and the doing and hyperactivity took over. This was another exchange of creation over the Creator. Jesus flipped over tables and drove out the religious people from a place that should have been all about God, worship, and ascribing great worth to the One who deserves it.

In the temple, God's people should have experienced a relationship with the Almighty, but instead, they received religion. Exhausting religion.

How have churches become a hangout for thieves today? When the focus is on church growth, buildings, production, personalities, great coffee, programs, and marketing – a place designed for God's glory can be dangerously hijacked. God's glory is exchanged for man's.

Most people can recite or mumble their way through the Lord's Prayer. Do you know what scripture follows the Lord's Prayer? Here's The Message Bible's translation of Luke 11:1-9:

"One day he was praying in a certain place. When he finished, one of his disciples said, "Master, teach us to pray just as John taught his disciples."

So he said,

"When you pray, say, Father, reveal who you are. Set the world right. Keep us alive with three square meals. Keep us forgiven with you and forgiving others. Keep us safe from ourselves and the Devil."

Then he said,

'Imagine what would happen if you went to a friend in the middle of the night and said, 'Friend, lend me three loaves of bread. An old friend traveling through just showed up, and I don't have a thing on hand.' The friend answers from his bed, 'Don't bother me. The door's locked; my children are all down for the night; I can't get up to give you anything.' 'But let me tell you, even if he won't get up because he's a friend, if you stand your ground, knocking and waking all the neighbors, he'll finally get up and get you whatever

you need. 'Here's what I'm saying: Ask and you'll get; Seek and you'll find; Knock and the door will open.'"

Jesus spoke and taught these words over 2,000 years ago. He taught young Jewish boys about prayer because they wanted to know how Jesus prayed. His prayers were different, and they were relational – real.

The young Jewish boys had been taught to pray three times a day. They had memorized rote, lengthy, religious prayers. They were affirmed and heralded as good Jewish boys for such dedication to prayer. But when they heard Jesus pray, they immediately knew their prayers, comparatively, were lame and lifeless. They asked Jesus to teach them how to pray as He prayed.

Today, people ask the same question: Can someone teach me how to pray? It makes no difference whether a person is a believer or not. People everywhere pray and want to know how to pray – effectively. Studies reveal that over 85% of Americans pray, yet most don't believe they know what they're doing. "Lord, how do we pray?"

The first church in the New Testament was dedicated to prayer (Acts 2:4). The church grew massively. On opening day, it grew to 3,000. The church multiplied greatly... 5,000, 10,000. Huge! According to Acts chapter six, internal problems had crept up within this growing church. Benevolent food distribution became unmanageable and required a meeting of the minds. The church leaders came together and appointed seven men to tackle the issue.

Church leaders believed capable men could handle the day-to-day logistics so that the spiritual leaders could focus on prayer, the Word, and worship. The ministry of prayer and the Word occupied most of the first church leaders' time, and because of this, the church thrived.

Let's Get Practical

We want to inspire others to live a life of passionate worship. According to Eugene Peterson, the central task of pastoral ministry is to teach people to pray.[19] Additionally, worship is a form of prayer, and prayer is a form of worship. And by the way, if you follow that – arguments about "style of worship" begin to fall by the wayside.

To develop into a praying church, we must first become a church of praying leaders. We understand leaders can only lead people so far in worship and prayer as they've been there themselves.

---

19 Peterson, Eugene H., A Long Obedience in the Same Direction: Discipleship in an Instant Society, Inter Varsity Press, Downers Grove, IL (1980)

Our weekly staff meetings involve much prayer. We want more prayer than planning, knowing that planning is very important. As staff and leaders, we model and teach people to pray with each other over the phone and in the hallways as soon as someone voices a prayer need.

How often do people express a prayer request, and someone says, "Yes, I'll pray for you," but they never do? No more! We want to pray with people right then and there. Now. Let's go. Let's pray!

Our Elder Team meetings have a decided focus on prayer and the Word. This paradigm shift has moved from long agenda-driven meetings to relational meetings where we experience God. We feel God leads His church better this way, and this is more sustainable for our church leaders and elders. Our elders also meet on Wednesday mornings for a prayer Zoom and meet on Sunday mornings to pray over and anoint the morning's speaker.

We will teach often about prayer. We will have prayer series and classes. We ask and train our church folks to write their prayer requests on our response cards so that staff and elders can pray specifically for people.

We have developed a prayer team of great intercessors – people with great spiritual gifts enabling them to lead in prayer. Our team prays together on Sunday mornings. They also lead our Community Night of Prayer on the third Thursday of each month. During this special monthly gathering, people come to our building for prayer, healing, comfort, miracles, and God. This is a powerful time of prayer for our church and community.

We want to offer prayer and worship opportunities. We provide nights of worship about once a quarter. We'll do weeks of 24/7 prayer in our auditorium. We have built more time for prayer, worship, and experiencing God into our Sunday worship gatherings.

And here's a caveat to all of this. It takes time.

Our services are no longer a clean, slick, one-hour production. We are taking time to read the Word, worship, pray, come to the altar, have communion, celebrate baptism, and teach expositorily through the Bible.

Our services range from an hour and fifteen minutes to an hour and a half. Are you OK with that? You may not beat the church crowd to Longhorn!

We think our intentional efforts honor God. We believe we are leading in ways that ascribe great worth to God. We hope our efforts spill over into the every day, as-you-go lives of those who call Lifebridge their home. We hope people are becoming living sacrifices—living all of life as worship.

What Can You Do To Connect People To God Through Prayer And Worship?

At the risk of sounding cliche, we encourage you to fall in love with Jesus. This may sound like an idea that is nothing more than a cheesy coffee mug or t-shirt.

Please remember that our pursuit as a church is one of relationship, not religion. Jesus did not come to start a religion. Instead, he came, lived, died, and resurrected to give us a living relationship with our Creator Father.

Your thirst for Jesus, like a deer panting for water, is vital. Sitting quietly with Jesus, the Word, and in worship in the morning or evening is a life-giving exercise. Your time with Jesus is essential to helping others connect to God through prayer and worship.

Gauge your time with Jesus compared to last year and maybe five years ago. Do you journal? What a great way to see and gauge your heart year after year. Are you listening to great, theologically sound, Gospel-driven worship music? If you're unsure where to find some excellent worship music, speak with our worship pastor.

How's your prayer life? Is it all words, making your prayers a one-way conversation with God? Do you sit and listen for His voice? Do you sit quietly and meditate on God's Word – asking Him to speak and guide you?

Who are the people around you, and do they encourage your prayer and worship? Do you encourage theirs? Are you in a Lifegroup (small group) where prayer, the Word, and worship are central?

And what about Sundays? Are you preparing for our worship gatherings on Saturday nights? Do you come early to church? We often play a pre-worship song to warm the place even before we start. You should get to church early! You should love on, greet, and prepare to worship with those around you. Consider how you will respond during worship, prayer, and the Word. How will you move according to your wiring, and how the Spirit moves you?

To connect people to God through prayer and worship, you must be a person of prayer and worship.

Gauge your fear of God. It's where wisdom and connection with God begin. How would others regard your reverence and awe of God? Do your kids see your personal devotional life of prayer, the Word, and worship? Do you and your wife help manage each other's souls and relationships with God?

Finally, rest.

Do you?

When was the last time you considered a sabbath day? A sabbath day is not taking a break when you have things done and in order. A sabbath is a day (24 hours) taken to rest when things are undone so that you won't be.

You take a sabbath exactly when life is busy to remind yourself that God is in control and you are not. A sabbath is like tithing. Tithing tells God, "You will do more with my 90% than I could with my 100%." A sabbath tells God, "You can do more with my six days than I could do with my seven."

A sabbath enables you to rest from your work so you can work from your rest.

John Ortberg writes, "The soul seeks God with its whole being. Because it is desperate to be whole, the soul is God-smitten and God-crazy and God-obsessed. My mind may be obsessed with idols; my will may be enslaved to habits; my body may be consumed with appetites. But my soul will never find rest until it rests in God."[20]

You must slow your soul. The one thing you never see with Jesus is hurry. Ascribing worth to a great Creator cannot be done well when rushed. Quality prayer, time in the Word, and worship demand we unbusy our inner person. This is the hard

---

20 Ortberg, John, Soul Keeping: Caring for the Most Important Part of You, Zondervan, Grand Rapids, MI, (2014)

part of connecting to God through prayer and worship, but it's also the best part.

Everyone around you is in a hurry. How powerful will it be if you're not? And when those harried and hurried folks ask about your quiet strength, maybe you can connect them to God through prayer and worship.

Questions

1. Read Matthew 21:13. How can we ensure that our places of worship truly reflect a house of prayer and not become distracted by other activities or priorities?

2. Read Luke 11:1-9. How can the model of prayer that Jesus teaches in these verses transform how we approach our prayer lives and our relationship with God?

3. How important is worship in your life? Is there a difference between the church's prayer focus and your life?

4. Do you agree that many pastors are program-driven rather than prayer-driven? Why or why not? Why do you think this is the case?

5. Why do you think that time in corporate prayer has diminished in today's evangelical church services?

6. What is one thing you can do to improve in prayer, the Word, and worship?

Notes

Author's End Note

There is a tremendous need for giving credit where credit is due. Years ago, perhaps around 2000, I met Rick Stedman of Adventure Christian Church in Roseville, California. At a conference Rick led, I was first exposed to the riches of the four pistons stemming from Acts 2:42. Over the years, I have taught God's powerful 4-piston engine so much that I'm no longer sure what is Rick's and what is mine. Because of that, I want to give Rick great credit and thanks! Rick is a good, generous man – and quite accomplished. Take a look:

The founding pastor of Adventure Christian Church, Rick Stedman, has garnered recognition for his ministerial capabilities. In 1998, only four years after he established the church, he was honored with the Donald McGavran Church Planting Award, bestowed on those who exemplify innovation and leadership in newly formed ministries.

In 2005, the North American Christian Convention honored Rick Stedman with its Special Achievement Award, which acknowledges excellence in church guidance. His undergraduate alma mater, William Jessup University (formerly San Jose Bible College), also designated him an Alumnus of the Decade 1980s. Rick Stedman has spent nearly three decades in the clergy.

After being ordained at the First Christian Church in Thousand Oaks, California, he remained an Associate Pastor until 1987. From 1987 to 1993, Rick Stedman served as Pastor of Administration and Singles with Crossroads Christian Church in Corona, California. He stayed with that ministry until starting Adventure Christian Church in 1994.

As an experienced minister with a Master's degree in Philosophy from the Claremont Graduate School, Rick Stedman makes it a practice to explain the reasonableness of Christianity. He also shows his congregation how to apply the Bible's teachings to their daily lives.

Throughout his ministry, he abides by the principle that knowing God is life's greatest adventure. In addition to his pastoral duties, Rick Stedman has shared his faith-based message in scores of publications. The author of more than 50 articles dealing with spiritual matters, he has also written two books. His most recent, 31 Reasons to Believe God Exists, was published in 2011. The other, Pure Joy! The Positive Side of Single Sexuality, has been in print since 1993. In 2000, it was re-released under the title Your Single Treasure.[21]

---

21 https://about.me/rickstedman

About the Author

Alan Scott: Alan was born in Gallup, N.M., in 1960. He is married to his Bible College sweetheart, Sherry McCracken, and they live in Marietta, GA. Sherry is a para-pro at an elementary school in Powder Springs, GA. They have four married children and a growing number of grandchildren. Brooklyn married Jared Cox, and they have a son, Calvin. Jared is the Director of North Georgia Christian Camp in Clarksville, GA. Lauren married Seth Banks, and they both work at North Georgia Christian Camp. Morgan married Stephen Haddox, and they have a second grandchild (unborn and unnamed as of this publication). Morgan is an online school teacher, and Stephen is a physics major working in the solar industry. Michael married Penelope Velez; Michael is a full-time musician, and Penelope is a nanny.

Alan has led and consulted with Ohio, Georgia, Indiana, and Colorado churches. Over the years, Alan has served as a youth pastor, worship pastor, college campus pastor, traveling evangelist, and lead pastor. He and Sherry also recorded two albums, "Live It Or Forget It" and "Spiritual Eyes." As a worship pastor, Alan recorded two live worship albums with Northwest Christian Church in Acworth, GA, and two youth worship albums with the PLA Youth Ministry in Daviess County, Indiana. As an author, Alan's books include: "I Quit Being A Christian To Follow Jesus," "Welcome To The Hotel California: Finding What You're Looking For," "Miracle In A Cornfield… It's A God-Thing," and the soon to be released, "Fat Rabbits."

For more information, you may contact Alan at alanrayscott@yahoo.com.

Other books are available from the author on Amazon.com.

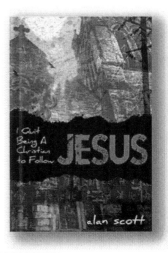

Lifebridgecommunity.com

Made in the USA
Columbia, SC
17 February 2025